CONTENTS

CURRICULUM LINKS

There are opportunities to explore a whole variety of curriculum links in *Snowman at Sunset*. All the songs link directly in with English as they involve learning about and using the English language. Try to find poems about snow and snowmen to expand this.

Here are some ideas to get you started:

SONG 1 **LOOK AT THE SNOWFLAKES**

Science: Explore and describe the way some everyday materials (such as water) change when they are heated or cooled.

Discuss the fact that every snowflake is different.

Communication, language and literacy:

Encourage the children to talk about how they feel when they see that it's snowing.

Art: Make paper snowflakes.

SONG 2 **WE'VE A SNOWMAN TO MAKE**

Personal, social and emotional development:

Use this song to discuss clothes and getting dressed.

SONG 3 **TEN TUBBY SNOWMEN**

Mathematics: This song will help practise saying and using number names in order.

Try to find other rhymes, songs and stories involving counting on and counting back.

Begin to relate subtraction to 'taking away'.

Look at number patterns and sequences.

SONG 4 **THE ANGRY SONG!**

English and drama:

Use language and actions to explore and convey different situations, characters and emotions.

Personal, social and emotional development:

Encourage children to share their feelings and talk about why they respond to experiences in particular ways.

SONG 5 **MISTER SUN**

Light and sound:

Discuss and identify different light sources, including the sun.

Knowledge and understanding of the world:

Look closely at differences and change. For example, the sun makes the snow look different (shiny and sparkly) and it makes my face feel warm.

SONG 6   THAT'S A JOB FOR US!

Personal, social and emotional development:

Use the story of *A Snowman at Sunset* to talk about the benefits of being able to work together harmoniously.

Involve children in identifying issues and finding solutions, encouraging them to think about the point of view of others.

Mathematics: Create 2 and 3D shapes.

This could link also with design and technology: make a papier mâché snowman.

Link science, maths and art:

All the children could contribute in making a collage for the classroom wall: for example, a large snowman with an oblong body, a circular head, square buttons, a hat comprising of a rectangle with a square on top, circular eyes and triangles for the nose and mouth. At one side, a blue sky with a few clouds from which 'Mister Sun' peeps; on the other side, a sunset. There can be snow on the ground around the snowman, which can sparkle under the light of the sun if glitter is used. *This can also be used as the backdrop for the play.*

SONG 7   A SNOWMAN AT SUNSET

Knowledge and understanding of the world:

Look closely at similarities, differences, pattern and change: what can happen at sunset? The sky can change colour, reds, pinks, oranges, etc.

Light and sound:

An opportunity to discuss that darkness is the absence of light.

CHARACTER LIST

Narrator   Can be read by a teacher, or split between a group of pupils.

10 Children   For small schools there could be as few as four children, who double up for actions in Song 4 THE ANGRY SONG and Song 6 THAT'S A JOB FOR US. They could also be positioned in the choir for Song 1 to help boost the singing. Three children are needed to speak lines.

10 Snowmen   Snow Mummy
Snow Daddy
Snow Granny
Snow Grandad
6 Snow Children

Sun   A short part with just a few lines.

STAGING

See curriculum links for backdrop suggestion.

The choir could stand to the right of the stage, in front of a background of paper snowflakes that the children have made themselves. The main characters could perform in front of and to the left of the choir.

SCRIPT AND SONG LYRICS

NARRATOR   Every year, the children waited. What do you think they were waiting for? Something very, very white, and very, very cold. Something which is good for fun and games…

Yes, that's it! The snow!

Song 1. LOOK AT THE SNOWFLAKES

1   Look at the snowflakes falling down,
Falling, falling.
Look at the snowflakes falling down,
From heaven to the ground.

2   Look at the snowflakes on the trees,
Soft and white, soft and white.
Look at the snowflakes on the trees,
They keep on falling down.

3   Look at the snowflakes on my nose,
Cold and clean, cold and clean.
Look at the snowflakes on my nose,
They keep on falling down.

4   Look at the snowflakes on my tongue,
Melting, melting.
Look at the snowflakes on my tongue,
They keep on falling down.

NARRATOR	Each year the snow fell until everywhere was covered in a beautiful, white carpet. Then the children could go sledging, throw snowballs and make enormous, deep white footprints. But most of all they loved making snowmen!
CHILDREN	Let's go and make a snowman now! *(Ten children come to centre stage)*

Song 2. WE'VE A SNOWMAN TO MAKE

1   Get your gloves and put them on,
    Your right hand then your left.
    Then we can go and play in the snow,
    We've a snowman to make!

2   Get your boots and put them on,
    Your right foot then your left.
    Then we can go and play in the snow,
    We've a snowman to make!

3   Get your coat and put it on,
    Your right arm then your left.
    Then we can go and play in the snow,
    We've a snowman to make!

4   Get your hat and put it on,
    It's cosy on your head.
    Then we can go and play in the snow,
    We've a snowman to make!

5   Get your scarf and put it on,
    It's cosy round your neck.
    Then we can go and play in the snow,
    We've a snowman to make!

NARRATOR

(The narrator pauses between each line to allow each snow character to enter. They form a line)
Each year, the children were lucky: there was always such a lot of snow, enough to make a whole family of snowmen:
… a snow mum…
… a snow dad…
… a snow granny…
… a snow grandad…
…and lots of snow children!
But then, after a few days, the sun would start to shine and the snow family would melt slowly away.

Song 3. TEN TUBBY SNOWMEN

1   There were *ten* tubby snowmen standing in a row,
The sun started shining and what do you suppose?
Two tubby snowmen said 'Phew, it's hot!'
Then they disappeared completely
'Cause they'd melted on the spot!

2   There were *eight* tubby snowmen…

3   There were *six* tubby snowmen…

4   There were *four* tubby snowmen…

5   There were *two* tubby snowmen…

NARRATOR

Then, one year, the children waited and waited for the snow. They waited for a long time. They thought that it would never, ever come.

It began to snow at last, but this year there was only enough to make ONE snowman. All the children wanted to use the snow! They ALL wanted to make a snowman!

CHILD 1	I want to make a snowman!
CHILD 2	No, I want to make a snowman!
CHILD 3	Actually, I want to make a snowman!
NARRATOR	The children got very angry with each other!

Song 4. THE ANGRY SONG!

1   This is a very cross song!
   This is an angry song!
   I saw someone stamp their feet,
*   *(Stamp, stamp, stamp)*
   Oh dear, what an angry song!

2   This is a very cross song!
   This is an angry song!
   I saw someone pull a face,
*   ('Ner, ner, ner!')
   Oh dear, what an angry song!

3   This is a very cross song!
   This is an angry song!
   I heard someone shouting out,
*   ('It's not fair!')
   Oh dear, what an angry song!

4   This is a very cross song!
   This is an angry song!
   I heard someone cry and cry,
*   ('Boo, hoo, hoo!')
   Oh dear, what an angry song!

* Two children only

The children sit down and look miserable.

NARRATOR	From behind the clouds, a pale yellow sun began to shine. The sun got warmer and warmer and the snow began to sparkle.

Song 5. MISTER SUN

1 You're peeping at me from under the clouds,
Under the clouds, under the clouds.
You're peeping at me from under the clouds,
Hello, Mister Sun!

2 You're shining on me from up in the sky,
Up in the sky, up in the sky.
You're shining on me from up in the sky,
Hello, Mister Sun!

3 You're making the snow look shiny and new,
Shiny and new, shiny and new.
You're making the snow look shiny and new,
Hello, Mister Sun!

4 You're making my face feel rosy and warm,
Rosy and warm, rosy and warm.
You're making my face feel rosy and warm,
Hello, Mister Sun!

© 2001 Out of the Ark Ltd, Surrey KT12 4RQ

NARRATOR	The sun looked down at the children.
SUN	Don't be angry with each other: try to be friends. You must make your snowman soon, or I will have to melt the snow.
CHILD 1	But which of us should make it?
SUN	All of you can make it. You can all work together.
NARRATOR	The children thought about this for a little while, then they decided what to do.

SONG 6. THAT'S A JOB FOR US!

1 We can make the snowman's *body*,
That's a job for us!
Fingers tingling in the snow,
There's a job to do, so off we go!

2 We can make the snowman's *head*…

3 We can find the snowman's *eyes*…

4 We can find the snowman's *nose*…

5 We can find the snowman's *mouth*…

© 2001 Out of the Ark Ltd, Surrey KT12 4RQ

NARRATOR   The children made the best snowman ever! They thought that making him together was great fun! The sun began to sink in the sky. He hadn't melted their snow after all. Ten tired children looked at their snowman, standing tall and proud against the sunset.

SONG 7. A SNOWMAN AT SUNSET

(First time solo) A snowman at sunset
And tired, sleepy children,
A snowman at sunset,
But now it's time for bed.
Maybe tomorrow, he will still be here,
One snowman at sunset this year.

All repeat the song

One snowman at sunset this year.

© 2001 Out of the Ark Ltd, Surrey KT12 4RQ

Reprise Song 1 for a rousing finale

10

Look At The Snowflakes

Words & Music:
NIKI DAVIES

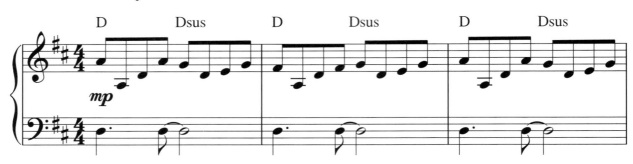

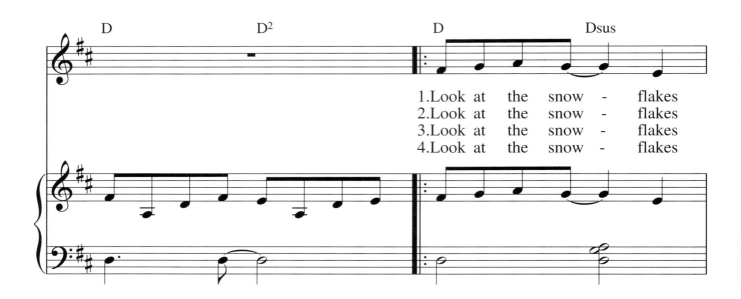

1.Look at the snow - flakes
2.Look at the snow - flakes
3.Look at the snow - flakes
4.Look at the snow - flakes

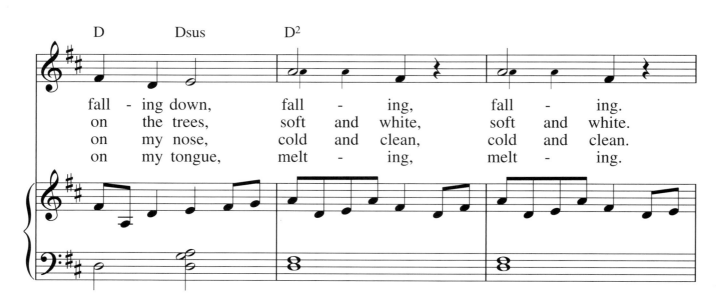

fall - ing down,   fall - ing,   fall - ing.
on the trees,   soft and white,   soft and white.
on my nose,   cold and clean,   cold and clean.
on my tongue,   melt - ing,   melt - ing.

Look at the snow - flakes fall - ing down from hea - ven to the
Look at the snow - flakes on the trees, they keep on fall - ing
Look at the snow - flakes on my nose, they keep on fall - ing
Look at the snow - flakes on my tongue, they keep on fall - ing

ground.
down.
down.
down.

1,2,3.   4.

13

We've A Snowman To Make

Words & Music:
NIKI DAVIES

Brightly ♩ = 164

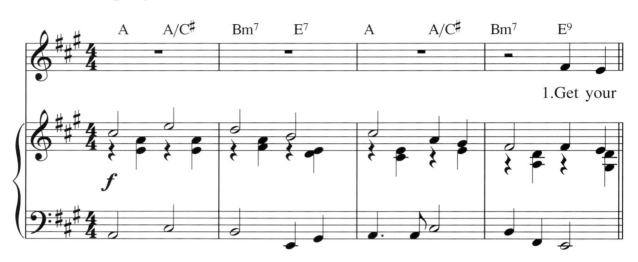

1.Get your

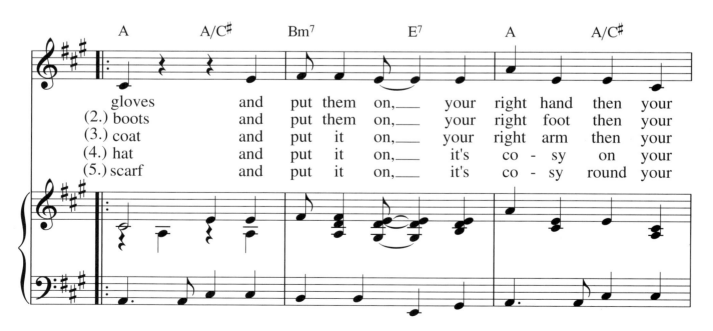

gloves and put them on,___ your right hand then your
(2.) boots and put them on,___ your right foot then your
(3.) coat and put it on,___ your right arm then your
(4.) hat and put it on,___ it's co - sy on your
(5.) scarf and put it on,___ it's co - sy round your

CCLI Song No. 4372712

15

Ten Tubby Snowmen

Words & Music:
NIKI DAVIES

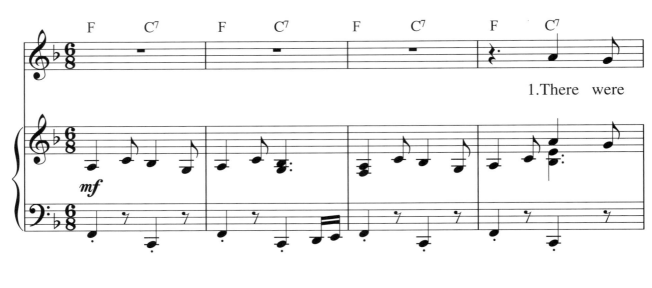

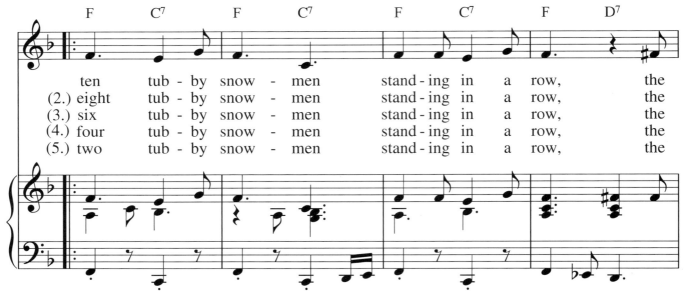

ten tub-by snow-men stand-ing in a row, the
(2.) eight tub-by snow-men stand-ing in a row, the
(3.) six tub-by snow-men stand-ing in a row, the
(4.) four tub-by snow-men stand-ing in a row, the
(5.) two tub-by snow-men stand-ing in a row, the

sun start-ed shin - ing and what do you sup-pose?

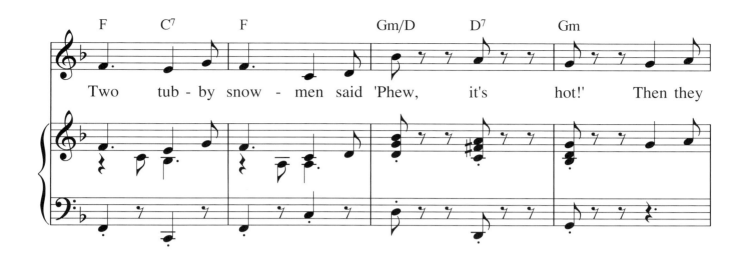

Two tub - by snow - men said 'Phew, it's hot!' Then they

1,2,3,4

dis - app - eared com - plete - ly 'cause they'd melt - ed on the spot!

5.

2. There were spot!
3. There were
4. There were
5. There were

The Angry Song!

Words & Music:
NIKI DAVIES

Defiantly ♩ = 146

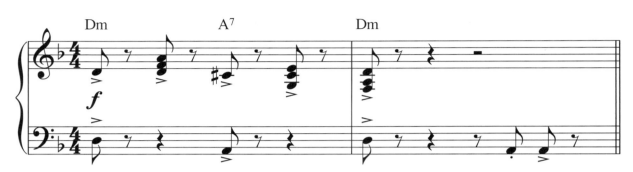

1. This is a ve-ry cross song! This is an
2. This is a ve-ry cross song! This is an
3. This is a ve-ry cross song! This is an
4. This is a ve-ry cross song! This is an

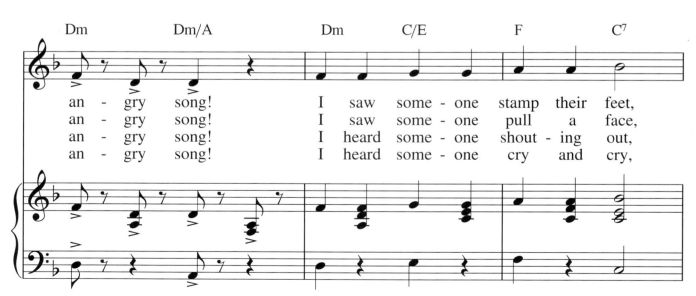

an - gry song! I saw some - one stamp their feet,
an - gry song! I saw some - one pull a face,
an - gry song! I heard some - one shout - ing out,
an - gry song! I heard some - one cry and cry,

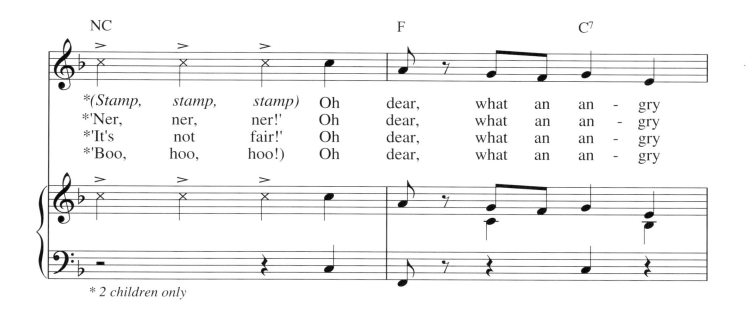

*(Stamp,   stamp,   stamp)   Oh   dear,   what   an   an - gry
*'Ner,   ner,   ner!'   Oh   dear,   what   an   an - gry
*'It's   not   fair!'   Oh   dear,   what   an   an - gry
*'Boo,   hoo,   hoo!)   Oh   dear,   what   an   an - gry

*2 children only

1,2,3.

4.

song!   song!
song!
song!

Mister Sun

Words & Music:
NIKI DAVIES

Relaxed ♩. = 56

20

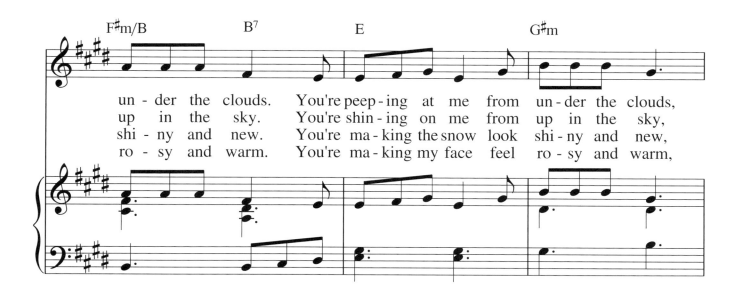

un - der the clouds. You're peep - ing at me from un - der the clouds,
up in the sky. You're shin - ing on me from up in the sky,
shi - ny and new. You're ma - king the snow look shi - ny and new,
ro - sy and warm. You're ma - king my face feel ro - sy and warm,

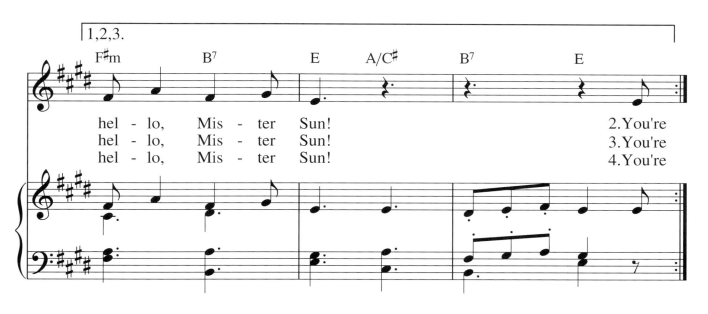

1,2,3.

hel - lo, Mis - ter Sun!
hel - lo, Mis - ter Sun!
hel - lo, Mis - ter Sun!

2.You're
3.You're
4.You're

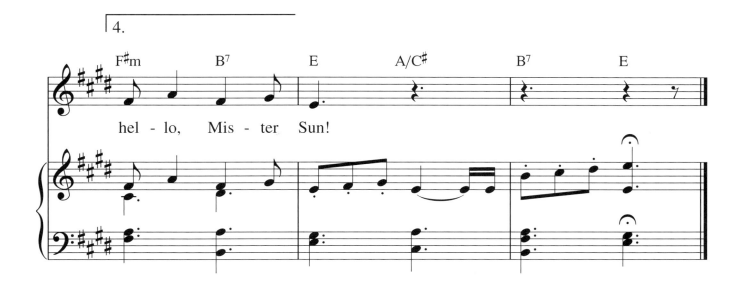

4.

hel - lo, Mis - ter Sun!

That's A Job For Us!

Words & Music:
NIKI DAVIES

Energetically ♩ = 168

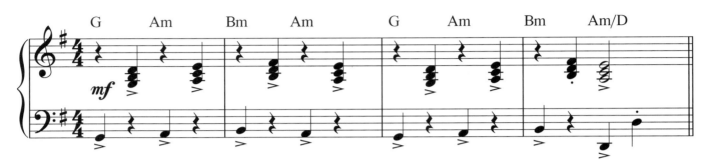

1.We can make the snow - man's bo - dy, that's a job for
2.We can make the snow - man's head, that's a job for
3.We can find the snow - man's eyes, that's a job for
4.We can find the snow - man's nose, that's a job for
5.We can find the snow - man's mouth, that's a job for

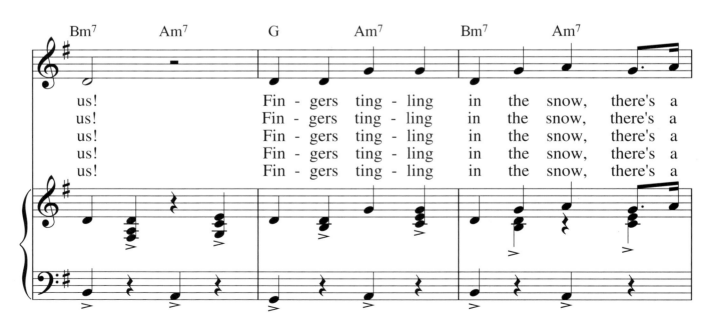

us! Fin - gers ting - ling in the snow, there's a
us! Fin - gers ting - ling in the snow, there's a
us! Fin - gers ting - ling in the snow, there's a
us! Fin - gers ting - ling in the snow, there's a
us! Fin - gers ting - ling in the snow, there's a

job to do, so off we go!
job to do, so off we go!
job to do, so off we go!
job to do, so off we go!
job to do, so off we

go!

Snowman At Sunset

Words & Music:
NIKI DAVIES

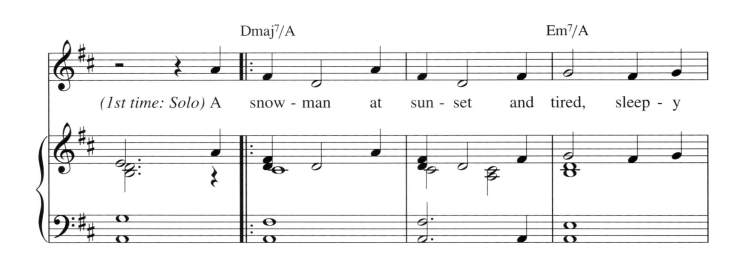

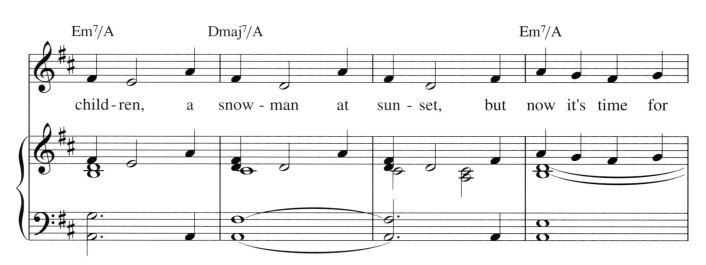

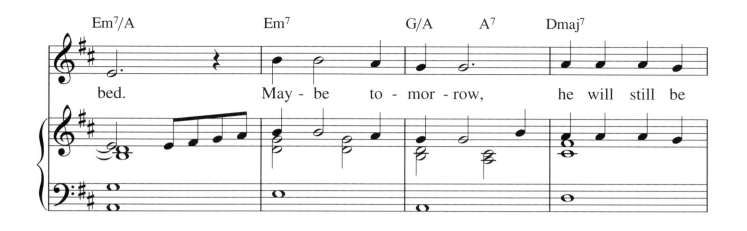

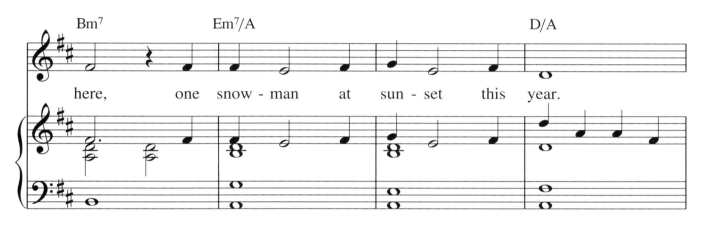

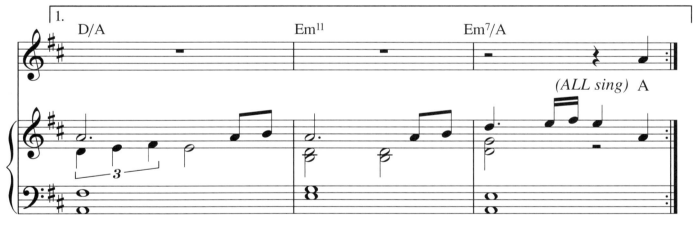

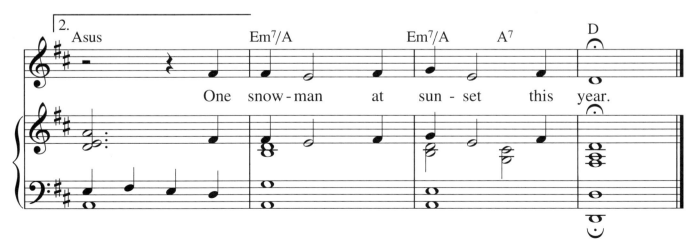

LICENCE APPLICATION FORM
(Snowman At Sunset)

If you perform *Snowman At Sunset* to an audience other than children and staff you will need to photocopy and complete this form and return it by post or fax to Out of the Ark Music in order to apply for a licence. If anticipated audience sizes are very small or if special circumstances apply please contact Out of the Ark Music.

The licence will permit the holder to:

- Perform *Snowman At Sunset* on the dates applied for.
- Reproduce the lyrics to the songs on printed paper, such as for programmes, and to make transparencies for overhead projection. The following credit should be included: *'Reproduced by kind permission © Out of the Ark Ltd'*.
- Photocopy the script for learning purposes. Copies must be destroyed after the performance.
- Make no more than two copies of the music, to be used by participating musicians on the performance dates.

If the performance is to be recorded please contact Out of the Ark Music.

We wish to apply for a licence to perform *Snowman At Sunset* by Niki Davies

Customer number (if known): ....

Name of school / organisation: ....

Name of organiser / producer: ....

Date(s) of performance(s): ....

Invoice address: ....

....

Post code: .... **Country:** ....

Telephone number: ....

Number of performances (excl. dress rehearsal)	Performances without admission charges	Performances with admission charges
1	☐ £11.75* [€17.50]	☐ £18.80 [€28.00]
2 or more	☐ £18.80 [€28.00]	☐ £23.50 [€35.00]

Tick one of the boxes above.

☐ Tick here if you wish to make an audio or video recording of the performance.

Tick one of the four payment options below: (Invoices will be sent with all licences)

☐ Please bill my school/nursery at the above address (UK schools/nurseries only)

☐ I enclose a cheque (Pounds Sterling) for £ .... payable to Out of the Ark Music

☐ I enclose a cheque (Euro) for € .... payable to Out of the Ark Music

☐ Please charge the following card: (Visa [not Electron], MasterCard, Maestro & American Express accepted)

Card No ....

Start Date _ _ / _ _ (MM/YY)   Expiry Date _ _ / _ _ (MM/YY)   3 digit security code: _ _ _ (last 3 digits on signature strip)

Address:	Out of the Ark Music	Phone:	+44 (0)1932 232250
	Sefton House	Fax:	+44 (0)1932 703010
	2 Molesey Road	Email:	info@outoftheark.com
	Hersham		
	Surrey KT12 4RQ		
	United Kingdom		

*The licence fees shown on this form are for 2008–2009 and may be subject to revision. All prices include VAT. Customers outside the EU will NOT be charged VAT.

COPYRIGHT & LICENSING

The world of copyright and licensing can seem rather daunting. Whilst it is a legal requirement for schools to comply with copyright law, we recognise that teachers are extremely busy. For this reason we try to make the process of compliance as simple as possible. The guidelines below explain the most common copyright and licensing issues.

Helpful information can be found on the following website:

> **A Guide to Licensing Copyright in Schools**
> **www.licensing-copyright.org**

And remember, we are always happy to help. For advice simply contact our customer services team:
UK: 01932 232 250   International: +44 1932 232 250   copyright@outoftheark.com

---

GENERAL GUIDELINES

You are free to use the material in our songbooks for all **teaching purposes**. However the **performance** of musicals or songs to an audience and the **reproduction** of scripts, lyrics and music scores are subject to licensing requirements by law. The key points are set out below:

PERFORMANCE OF MUSICALS

The performance of works involving drama, movement, narratives or spoken dialogue requires a specific licence from the publisher. ****Your PRS licence does not cover musicals****

We issue affordable licences to schools, churches and nurseries and to simplify the process we include a licence application form with all of our musicals and nativity plays. This can be photocopied and posted or faxed to us.

> #### The performance licence will permit the holder to:

- Perform the musical on the dates applied for.
- Reproduce the song lyrics on printed paper, e.g. for programmes; to make transparencies for overhead projection and to display the lyrics on an interactive whiteboard or other type of screen. The following credit should be included with the lyrics:
  'Reproduced by kind permission © Out of the Ark Ltd'.
- Photocopy the script for learning purposes. Copies must be destroyed after the performance.
- Make no more than two photocopies of the music score, to be used by participating musicians on the performance dates.

AUDIO AND VIDEO RECORDINGS

If you wish to make an audio or video recording of any of our works please contact us directly:

UK: 01932 232 250   International: +44 1932 232 250   copyright@outoftheark.com

---

Other use of the published material

If you are not staging the musical but still intend to use material from the publication then different licences are required:

Reproduction of Song Lyrics or Musical Scores

The following licences from Christian Copyright Licensing Ltd (www.ccli.com) permit photocopying or reproduction of song lyrics and music scores, for example to create song-sheets, overhead transparencies or to display the lyrics or music using any electronic display medium.

For UK schools: A Collective Worship Copyright Licence and a Music Reproduction Licence.
For churches: A Church Copyright and Music Reproduction Licence.

Please ensure that you log the songs that are used on your copy report. (Organisations that do not hold one of the above licences should contact Out of the Ark Music directly for permission.)

Performance of Songs

If you are not staging a musical but are performing any of our songs for the public on school premises (i.e. for anybody other than staff and pupils) then royalty payments become due. Most schools have an arrangement with the Performing Rights Society (PRS) through their local authority. Organisations that do not have such an arrangement should contact Out of the Ark Music directly.

SEASONAL SONG COLLECTIONS

by Niki Davies

From one of Britain's top music writers for children, this series of seasonal collections from Niki Davies provides a wonderful library of songs that are simple to learn and great fun to sing – an ideal resource for use throughout the year!

Written for nursery and reception aged children, but suitable for older children too, each book contains ten songs along with lots of ideas for further activities and curriculum links.

Each songbook package provides:

- Quality recordings of all the songs, sung by children
- Professionally arranged and produced backing tracks
- Piano music with melody, lyrics and guitar chords
- Teachers' notes/curriculum links for The Foundation Stage

IT MUST BE SPRING!

With ten brand new songs for springtime and other times of the year, this songbook will be an instant hit with younger children.

Titles include:

- It must be spring!
- Somebody's waking up
- It's Mother's Day
- Wet, wet, wet!
- Where did the pancake go?
- A tiny seed was sleeping

HAPPY SUN HIGH

A superb collection of songs for summer and throughout the year, this book includes ten enchanting songs to brighten up everyone's day whatever the weather!

Titles include:

- Come with me to the beach
- Sunglasses
- Caterpillar
- Steam train
- Picnic
- Lying in the daisies

IT'S TIME TO FLY

Children will adore these ten original songs for autumn, with words and melodies that beautifully capture the changes of the season.

Titles include:

- One, two, three little acorns
- The owl
- Pumpkin head
- Mr Scarecrow
- Autumn leaves
- Under the harvest moon

IT'S WINTER TIME

Providing plenty of material for those winter days, with songs about frosty mornings, keeping warm and Christmas preparations, this book is an ideal supplementary resource for any winter term projects.

Titles include:

- Marching in the snow
- Snowdrop
- Put your coat on
- Jack Frost
- Mister Wind
- Socks

Out of the Ark Music, Sefton House, 2 Molesey Road, Hersham Green, Surrey KT12 4RQ, UK
Telephone 01932 232250, Fax 01932 703010
Email info@outoftheark.com
www.outoftheark.com